Profound View,
Fearless Path

The Bodhisattva Vow

Profound View, Fearless Path

The Bodhisattva Vow

by

Dzogchen Ponlop
Rinpoche

SIDDHI PUBLICATIONS
Vancouver, Canada 2000

SIDDHI PUBLICATIONS
P.O. Box 93542
RPO Nelson Park
Vancouver, British Columbia
Canada
V6E 4L7

E-mail:
siddhipubs@nalandabodhi.org

PROFOUND VIEW, FEARLESS PATH
©1999 by Dzogchen Ponlop Rinpoche
(Formerly entitled
THE BODHISATTVA VOW)
All Rights Reserved.

ISBN 0-9687689-4-6

Second edition August 2000

PROFOUND VIEW, FEARLESS PATH

The Bodhisattva Vow

Contents

PROFOUND VIEW, FEARLESS PATH
The Bodhisattva Vow

INTRODUCTION

Taking the Bodhisattva Vow means that we are going to engage in the procedures for initially generating Bodhicitta, the mind of awakening. Generally speaking, the individual liberation vows of the Hinayana tradition are transmitted in a coarse manner by means of a signal. In the case of the Refuge Vow, as well as in the case of novice and full ordinations, the signal is a finger snap indicating the moment at which the vow or ordination is complete.

The transmission of the Bodhisattva Vow is more subtle; it is internal. The vow is accomplished through the force of the students' intention in taking it. Your attitude and intention are of the utmost importance in this process. Therefore, you must look at and examine your motivation.

It is necessary in the beginning to know the benefits and qualities of Bodhicitta. It is necessary to understand, basically, what Bodhicitta is. Then, when you actually take the vow and generate Bodhicitta formally, you do so within the recollection of these things.

The first thing that the generation of Bodhicitta depends upon is the presence of love and compassion directed towards all beings. The intention should be: "I will establish all beings, without exception, in a state of present happiness and ultimate happiness, and I will free all beings, without exception, from their present suffering and from all suffering." Possessing this as your intention and generating this as your attitude is the basis for receiving the vow.

THE TWO LINEAGES OF THE BODHISATTVA VOW

The Bodhisattva Vow is the entrance to the path of the Mahayana. The Bodhisattva Vow ceremony exists in two formats which come from the two lineages of the Mahayana transmission of this vow. One tradition is called the Lineage of Vast or Extensive Conduct. This format comes from Maitreya. It involves an extensive ceremony that requires two days to perform.

The other tradition is called the Lineage of the Profound View. This tradition began with Arya Nagarjuna. It was passed on from him to Chandrakirti, Shantideva, and so on up to the present. It is the one we're going to be doing. It does not involve a particularly dramatic ceremony. What has to be dramatic is your attitude because the Dharma is internal: It's in your mind. The actual words used as the liturgy of the vow were composed by the Bodhisattva Shantideva and are found in the *Bodhicaryavatara*.

ASPIRATION AND IMPLEMENTATION BODHICITTA

The attitude of the vow itself is two-fold. These two attitudes are called Aspiration Bodhicitta and Implementation Bodhicitta. If you are familiar with the Mahayana Dharma, then you will know about these and therefore it will be easy for you to generate Bodhicitta now.

Aspiration Bodhicitta is exactly what its name implies: It is the aspiration or desire for a certain result. It is an intention, a motivation. Because it is a thought, it is not difficult to generate. Its generation requires merely an alteration of your intention or attitude. While it is simple to generate in that way, it is extraordinarily and immeasurably beneficial. In this case, aspiration means a pure aspiration for the accomplishment of omniscient Buddhahood; not simply for yourself but in order to bring all beings without exception to that same state. That is the aspiration which is Aspiration Bodhicitta.

Three Styles of Aspiration Bodhicitta

There are three styles of Aspiration Bodhicitta. They are called King-like Bodhicitta, Ferryman-like Bodhicitta and Shepherd-like Bodhicitta. Any one of these three is sufficient for the development of authentic Aspiration Bodhicitta.

King-like Bodhicitta, as the name implies, is similar to the approach of a king. A king must first consolidate his authority and amass sufficient wealth. Thereafter, if he is a good king, he uses his authority to protect his kingdom and shares his wealth with his subjects. King-like Bodhicitta is similar. It is the thought, "In order to be able to free all beings, I must first accomplish all the qualities of Buddhahood. I must train in the path, acquire profound prajna and compassion, and attain awakening myself. Having done so, I will then use these qualities to bring all beings to that same state." That is King-like Bodhicitta. The idea is that you must attain Buddhahood first in order to be able to liberate others.

The second style is Ferryman-like or Boatman-like Bodhicitta. A ferryman seeks to bring himself and all of his passengers safely across the body of water at the same time. Similarly, someone who generates Ferryman-like Bodhicitta makes the aspiration, "I will bring all beings across the ocean of samsara with me so that all beings attain Buddhahood simultaneously."

The third style of Aspiration

Bodhicitta is Shepherd-like Bodhicitta. A shepherd first sends the flock out ahead of him and then follows after them to make sure that they are protected. In the evening, he sends them in ahead of him and then follows after them to make sure that they all return safely. So he is the last to arrive. He ensures that they have good grazing and protects the flock from wolves.

In the same way, someone who generates Shepherd-like Bodhicitta makes the aspiration that, through his practice, all other beings will be brought first to the attainment of full Buddhahood. One aspires to be the last being to accomplish the peace and happiness of Buddhahood.

Shepherd-like Bodhicitta is the thought, "My happiness is unimportant compared to the happiness of all beings, so may I drive all beings before me into awakening. May I remove all of their obstacles to awakening. May I be the last to attain Buddhahood." This type of Bodhicitta is exemplified by the Bodhisattva Avalokiteshvara; in particular, as illustrated in his form with one-thousand eyes and one thousand arms.

Shepherd-like Bodhicitta is the hardest for ordinary beings to generate because Bodhicitta is not just simply an idea or a fantasy but something that would actually be implemented in your experience. If we look at the way we act, we'll see why this really goes against the grain of our conventional personality. For example, when we're shopping and we have to line up at the cash register, we all want to be first. We don't let everyone else in the store go before us. Similarly, when we are waiting for a taxi, we take the first taxi that arrives in order to get to our destination without delay. We don't let the people who came to the taxi-stand after us take that first cab.

It's very hard for ordinary beings to truly generate this Bodhicitta. For that reason, the Buddha said it is supreme. Of these three types of Bodhicitta, the Buddha said that the best is Shepherd-like Bodhicitta, the second best is Ferryman-like Bodhicitta, and the third best is King-like Bodhicitta.

Any of these three is acceptable as authentic Aspiration Bodhicitta. You needn't try and talk yourself into Shepherd-like Bodhicitta if that's not the way you feel right now. You should generate whichever of the three suits your disposition at this time. In any case, the actual generation of Aspiration Bodhicitta is done by repeating the words which describe its generation. It is important that you consider the meaning while reciting because the essence of this vow is generated within your mind.

Implementation Bodhicitta

Following the generation of Aspiration Bodhicitta, one generates Implementation Bodhicitta. In fact, it can only be generated on the basis of Aspiration Bodhicitta. First, one has to generate the aspiration, "I will free all beings." On that basis, one can commit oneself to engaging in the practices and activities which are necessary to bring that aspiration to fruition. The form this takes is saying, "Just as all Buddhas and Bodhisattvas of the past have done, I will practice all aspects of the path of a Bodhisattva."

By generating Implementation Bodhicitta and committing oneself to the actual practice, one ensures that one's Aspiration Bodhicitta does not remain merely a dream. It makes certain that one will actually realize this dream.

In this Lineage of the Profound View, both Aspiration and Implementation Bodhicitta are generated in the same ceremony. Actually, they are generated at the same time. One says, "Just as all the Buddhas and Bodhisattvas of the past have generated Bodhicitta, I will generate Aspiration Bodhicitta. Just as they have trained in the various aspects of the path, I will train in the various aspects of the path."

In Shantideva's explanation, Aspiration Bodhicitta is like the intention to go to a particular destination. Implementation Bodhicitta is doing whatever you have to do to get there; such as getting an automobile and driving it to your destination, taking a train, or whatever. Obviously, if you don't have the intention to go to that destination, you won't do what is needed to get there. So both are needed. The intention and the process of actually going through with that intention depend upon each other. If you generate these two aspects of Bodhicitta, Aspiration and Implementation Bodhicitta, then your generation of Bodhicitta is complete.

COMMITMENTS OF THE
BODHISATTVA VOW

It is extremely important for you to understand the commitments of the Bodhisattva Vow before you undertake it. It is said traditionally in Tibet that with important things, "Be very careful." It was said by the panditas of India, in reference to matters of importance, "Repeat everything twice." Therefore, it is necessary to discuss the most important commitments in some detail. The particular format for this is a concise explanation that brings together the two traditions of the Profound View and Extensive Conduct.

The most important commitment of Aspiration Bodhicitta is, mentally, not to abandon sentient beings. This means that if you generate the intention not to help a sentient being, even if you can help that being, it goes against the Bodhisattva Vow. That means any one sentient being. It does not mean that to violate the Bodhisattva Vow you have to generate the attitude, "I will never help any sentient being," because no one could possibly generate that. It's just unheard of.

An example of violating the Bodhisattva Vow would be to develop the attitude, "I will establish all sentient beings in a state of complete Buddhahood, and do everything I can to help all sentient beings except for this one particular person, so and so." Leaving someone out of your Bodhisattva commitment is exactly the attitude that violates your Bodhisattva Vow. Generating the attitude, "Even if I get a chance to help this particular being, I will not," or perhaps, "If I get a chance to hurt this particular being, I will," is a violation of the Bodhisattva Vow; no matter who that particular being is.

Five Commitments of Aspiration Bodhicitta

In this explanation, there are a total of five commitments of Aspiration Bodhicitta. The first of these is the root commitment not to abandon sentient beings which we went over in such a pleasant way. That's the most important one. Then there is a set of three that go together and finally there is a fifth commitment.

The set of three are things to do. The first of the set of three is to accomplish conducive conditions; meaning to accomplish conditions conducive to the flourishing or growth of Bodhicitta. This refers to the recollection of the benefits of Bodhicitta. One should continually reflect on the benefits of Bodhicitta.

The second of this set of three is to accomplish the cause of the growth of Bodhicitta. The cause is the gathering of the two accumulations of merit and wisdom. In the beginning, one needs to accumulate merit in order to increase the power or intensity of one's mind of awakening. In the end, one needs to gather the two accumulations of merit and wisdom in order to perfect Bodhicitta.

The third of this set of three is to accomplish the methods by which Bodhicitta is increased. These methods are mind-training. Fundamentally, this means not to leave Bodhicitta behind in the shrine room but always to remain inseparable from it. Apply it again and again. Cultivate Bodhicitta by training your mind through such practices as taking and sending, the exchanging of oneself for others, and the recognition of the sameness or equality of oneself and others.

So those three, accomplishing conducive conditions, gathering merit and wisdom which is the cause, and accomplishing the methods of the increase of Bodhicitta are the second, third and fourth commitments. The fifth commitment is to abandon the causes of violating the Bodhisattva Vow, or losing Bodhicitta, through lying or otherwise deceiving sentient beings. This is known as abandoning the causes of the impairment of the vow.

The main causes of impairment are what are called the four evil things, or four bad things. Abandoning them will itself provide enhancement for Bodhicitta. The first of the four evil things is to deceive the Venerable; meaning one's teachers, the Three Jewels and so forth. The second is to regret what is not cause for regret. In other words, while it is appropriate to regret harmful actions, it is extremely inappropriate to regret virtuous actions. So the second evil thing is to regret one's practice of dharma or regret acts of virtue, such as acts of generosity. The third is to hate and wish for harm to come to a Bodhisattva through anger. The fourth is to deceive sentient beings. If we can avoid these four, then we will be able to protect the Bodhisattva Vow.

Commitments of Implementation Bodhicitta

To train in the Six Perfections is the commitment of Implementation Bodhicitta. When you take the Bodhisattva Vow, specifically when you generate the Bodhicitta of Implementation, you are committing yourself to the practice of the Six Perfections. This means that you are not thinking, "At some point in the future, when I'm able, I will practice the Six Perfections." Instead, you are committing yourself to their practice from now on.

When you commit yourself to training in or practicing the Six Perfections, this does not mean that you should expect your practice of them will be perfect and completely unmistaken from the beginning. That would not be the path: It would be the fruition. It is quite possible that you will make mistakes or that your training will be incomplete for some time. Nevertheless, you commit yourself to practicing. You commit yourself to actually practicing generosity; to actually maintaining moral discipline; to cultivating patience; to cultivating exertion or diligence; to practicing and generating meditative stability; and to developing prajna through hearing and contemplating as well as through analysis applications in meditation.

As we are ordinary beings, downfalls will arise almost continually. Therefore it's necessary to try to avert them. Nevertheless, one should not become overly discouraged when one experiences or incurs a downfall of the Bodhisattva Vow. It was said by Lord Atisha that violations of the Bodhisattva Vow occurred for him at the rate of dust falling on a clean table in a dusty country. You clean it and then, in the next minute, it's all covered with dust again. So you must clean it again and again and so forth. Lord Atisha said that although these downfalls come all the time, nevertheless, if you keep on cleaning then you can have a clean table.

Again, it is important not to become discouraged. Every time a downfall occurs, you simply purify or cleanse it with its recognition as a downfall, followed by confession and so forth.

Those are the main commitments
of the Bodhisattva Vow.

THE ROOT DOWNFALLS

There are two types of violations of the Bodhisattva Vow; the root downfalls and the branch transgressions. There are three explanations of the root downfalls. When it is explained for those of highest capability, there are fourteen. For those of medium capability, there are four. For those of lesser capability, there is one.

Explained as Fourteen

For those of the highest capability, the fourteen downfalls are divided into unusual categories. First are five that kings are at risk of performing. Then there is an additional one that ministers, in the sense of cabinet-level politicians, are at risk of performing. Finally, there are eight that everyone is at risk of performing.

The first of the five for kings is to steal or confiscate things offered to or belonging to the Three Jewels. The second is to forbid or prevent people from making offerings, or to cause them to refrain from making offerings. The third is to punish, in a secular or legal manner, those who have violated their religious discipline; such as violating monastic rules or the discipline of a bodhisattva.

The fourth is to perform one of the five actions of immediate consequence: patricide, the killing of one's father; matricide, the killing of one's mother; killing an arhat; causing a schism in the sangha; or drawing blood from a buddha with a malevolent intention. Performing any of the five actions of immediate consequence is the fourth downfall. However, causing a schism and drawing blood from a Buddha with malevolent intention cannot happen now. The schism referred to here is described as between the original teacher, the Buddha, and his sangha. So while the real schism cannot happen now, a similar schism can happen when you separate students either from the teacher or into two groups.

The fifth downfall is to have and propagate wrong views. Wrong view means, in this context, holding and propagating the view that there is no moral cause and result. It is the view that there is no such thing as karma.

At the time the scriptures were taught, there was a greater possibility for the king to commit these five. This is because the mentality of a king is very different. When you are in that position in society, you have such complete power. If some little thing goes wrong and you get mad, it is very easy to get rid of the problem: You just kill it. If a king were to get a little mad about the Buddha, he could just say: "Kill him." The same thing could happen if he were to get mad at an arhat or his parents. There are stories in every country of kings who killed their fathers in order to gain their fathers' seats as king. So even parents got scared of their sons.

Originally it was easier for a king to commit these five downfalls. It is only now that we ordinary beings are becoming more engaged with these five. So now it also applies to us.

The sixth downfall is the one particular to ministers: It is to destroy cities. The destruction of cities refers to an act of war exerted against a civilian population. While ministers can also commit any of the first five, the sixth one is a particular danger for people in a ministerial position in government.

The remaining downfalls are

easy for a beginner to commit. The seventh root downfall is to teach emptiness to those who are unprepared to hear it or to those who are untrained. Unprepared or untrained here means those whose acumen or intellectual understanding has not been sharpened to the point where they can appreciate or understand emptiness.

It is a fact that emptiness is hard to hear about. For that reason, genuine teachers do not teach about emptiness casually. There is a story in the sutras that once, from among the people receiving instruction from Arya Manjushri on the Mahayana doctrine of emptiness, there were 500 Hinayana practitioners of the Shravaka family. These 500 people had heart-attacks and died.

In fact, we are not in much danger of incurring this root downfall. One who does not understand emptiness does not incur this downfall by explaining emptiness to those who also do not understand it. Just as we are ourselves not understanding emptiness, neither delighted nor terrified by it, so also those to whom we might casually explain it would be neither delighted nor terrified. This root downfall occurs when someone who understands and has realized emptiness explains it to someone who is capable of understanding emptiness, but is not yet ready to hear it. Getting a glimpse of it, they are terrified.

The eighth downfall is to turn someone away from the path of awakening. This is to tell an individual who, having generated the mind of awakening, is engaged to some degree in the practice of the path, "This Mahayana is extremely difficult; someone like you could not possibly practice it! You had better drop it." If you discourage them in this way and, based on your advice, they either revert to the Shravakayana or to a non-dharmic approach to life, then you have committed this downfall.

The ninth downfall is similar: It is to turn a Hinayana practitioner away from the practice of Hinayana. There are people who are naturally suited for the practice of the lesser vehicle. Practicing the greater vehicle will not be of particular benefit to them.

Suppose you go to such a person and say, "The Shravakayana is very low and very inferior. It is of no benefit. You should give it up and practice Mahayana, or just give up practice altogether." If you say this to such a person and cause them to enter into the Mahayana or into a non-dharmic path, then you have committed this root downfall. It is committed even if you cause them to enter into the Mahayana because they will not be able to practice it. You have turned them away from what is, for them, an appropriate path.

The tenth downfall is having wrong views about the Hinayana. If you generate a belief that the Hinayana is totally ineffective and that one cannot attain liberation by it, or that one cannot abandon mental affliction, ego-clinging, by means of the Hinayana, and especially if you proclaim it to others, that is the tenth root downfall of a Bodhisattva.

The eleventh downfall is to praise yourself and criticize others in order to acquire material possessions or respect. Principally this refers to a situation where the praise of oneself and criticism of others is not true. To say, "I am a great teacher of the Mahayana and an excellent monk but that other guy over there is a bad teacher and a very poor monk" is an example of this kind of root downfall.

The twelfth downfall is to pretend to have realized something profound about dharma when you have not. This refers to actual pretense; not the case of self-deception. The motivation for pretense is to maintain or acquire a certain position and so forth. For instance, if I were to say, "I have directly realized the truth of the nature of all things, which is emptiness," then I would incur this root downfall, because it so happens that I have not. This downfall is particularly a danger for practitioners of Vajrayana. If one says, "I just met this yidam," and one did not, or "My yidam said to me the other day such and such," and they didn't, then you have incurred this root downfall.

The thirteenth downfall is to cause punishment to occur for either a Bodhisattva of the Mahayana, or a bhikshu or monk of the Hinayana, by making a false accusation to a person in authority in order to solidify your own position or to acquire new things. Punishment here could be in a legal context. It could also be punishment in a religious context; such as the loss of position within a religious community. In actual fact, it is when you bribe someone in a position of authority to cause some sort of legal or other action to be taken against a bodhisattva or bhikshu. For the root downfall to be complete, the actual punishment has to occur: The bribed official has to go through with it.

The fourteenth downfall is quite easy to understand. It is to steal the means of sustenance intended for or belonging to a renunciate meditator, and give them to someone else. The reason this is a root downfall is that by depriving the renunciate of the means of sustenance, you prevent that meditator from being able to remain in an isolated situation of meditation or retreat. There are a couple of variations of this. One is to steal the sustenance of a meditator and give it to a scholar or someone who is studying; the other is to steal the sustenance of a scholar and give it to someone who is not studying. Of these two, it is said to be a more severe downfall to steal the sustenance of a meditator.

Explained as Four

The explanation of root downfalls as fourfold is explained for Bodhisattvas of intermediate capability. These are the ones which are most commonly applied as a standard. This explanation contains everything we have to watch out for.

The first of these, to abandon bodhicitta, refers to the abandonment of Aspiration Bodhicitta. Abandoning the thought or intention, "For the benefit of all sentient beings, I will attain full awakening," or "I will establish all sentient beings in full awakening," is the first root downfall.

The second is to refrain from the practice of generosity out of attachment and greed. It means not giving something that you are well capable of giving. It refers both to dharma and to real possessions. In the case of dharma, if you possess the capability of explaining an aspect of dharma; encounter someone who wishes to receive an explanation of it; know that such an explanation will benefit them; have the intention to benefit them; and you do not give it out of greed or attachment, then you have committed this root downfall.

It is said in the text that even if someone comes knocking on your door at midnight, you should teach them what they want. With regard to material possessions, it is based on your own situation. It means not giving what you can afford to give.

The third is to become aggressive. It has a specific meaning in this context. It means that through one's anger, one becomes so aggressive or negative towards another person that you do not accept their apology. Even if they apologize repeatedly for whatever they have done that has made you angry, you continue to be angry. So this refers to a type of stable or deeply-felt anger which will not listen to any apology.

The fourth is dharmic pretense. It means that although you are filled with kleshas, and have not abandoned them at all, you pretend to have abandoned them. You pretend to be a bodhisattva or a bhikshu when you are not. You pretend that you have actually dealt with the kleshas when you have not, and you pretend to have real qualities that you do not possess. It does not refer to trying to modify your conduct when your emotional state is unstable. The point of this is that it is necessary to be straightforward and honest about your own situation.

Explained as One

The third explanation of the root downfalls as one is given for those of lesser faculties. The conduct being maintained is basically the same whether it is described as fourteen or four or one. It is the simplicity of the explanation that is different. In the case of this one, the root downfall is to abandon the bodhicitta of aspiration. It is to abandon the intention to benefit sentient beings and the intention to bring all sentient beings to awakening. This means that if one mentally abandons the welfare of any single sentient being at any time for any reason, this root downfall is incurred. As was discussed previously, if I were to think, "I will help all sentient beings and everyone here, but certainly not so and so, I will never help so and so," then I have incurred this root downfall.

If one takes the Bodhisattva Vow according to the Lineage of Profound View, then these are the root downfalls to be avoided. One can think of them as the fourteen, as the four, or as the one; it does not matter. Any of the three ways of considering or enumerating the downfalls of the Bodhisattva Vow is acceptable.

The Eighty Branch Transgressions

There are also the eighty branch defects or branch transgressions of the Bodhisattva Vow. It is not necessary to go through these in detail. The eighty branch defects consist of variations in a mathematical progression from two main defects. The two are multiplied by body, speech and mind, each of which is multiplied by whether it occurs in the past, present or future, and so forth. So although you end up with eighty, basically there are just two of them.

The first is to not pacify the physical suffering and mental misery of others when one is able to do so. The second is to not generate the physical pleasure and mental happiness of others when one is able to do so. These two turn into eighty by being multiplied by various factors, but in fact what is to be observed is just these two. It is unnecessary to go through them all as what is to be observed is essentially the two root ones. After those two, it is basically just a question of mathematics.

THE THREE-FOLD FEARLESSNESS OF A BODHISATTVA

As Shantideva uses the term "Bodhisattva," it can be applied to anyone who has taken the Bodhisattva Vow. It indicates that someone has generated this supreme and excellent intention of Bodhicitta and therefore is fit to be called a Bodhisattva. As Chandrakirti uses the term, it is only applied in the full sense when you're talking about someone on one of the ten levels of Bodhisattva realization. Here we are following Shantideva's usage of the term.

In Tibetan, the "sattva" part of the term Bodhisattva is translated as "sempa"; "sem" is mind and "pa" is courageous. If sempa is used in referring to a person, it means warrior. So Bodhisattva here means someone who has a courageous mind and a courageous intention to attain awakening.

The reason someone who takes the Bodhisattva Vow is fit to be called a Bodhisattva is that simply taking the vow involves a tremendous amount of courage. This is usually enumerated as a three-fold fearlessness.

The first fearlessness of a Bodhisattva is being unafraid of the number of beings for whom one is taking responsibility. You are accepting as your own individual responsibility the welfare and the eventual awakening of an inconceivable, possibly infinite, number of beings. I mean, think about it: It's hard enough to get along with a family of three people.

The second fearlessness of a Bodhisattva is that you are not discouraged by the length of time this is going to take. It is said in the Mahayana scriptures, for someone of the highest capacity, the shortest length of time on the path from the taking of the Bodhisattva Vow until one's full awakening is three periods of uncountable kalpas. Uncountable means the number which is ten to the power of sixty. Each of these uncountable kalpas has the duration of a galaxy. So, you're not afraid of that length of time on the path.

The third fearlessness is that you have no fear of the difficulty that the Bodhisattva Vow and Bodhisattva Path is going to entail. It entails difficulty because what you are committing yourself to do is pleasing other beings which is very, very hard to do. For example, once when the Buddha gave the Bodhisattva Vow, one of the people who took it was a monk. Having taken the Bodhisattva Vow, this monk went down the road and met a Brahmin. This Brahmin was not a normal Brahmin. He was an emanation of Mara, a demonic person sent to test and frustrate this poor monk. The Brahmin said to the monk, "I need a human hand. Will you please give me your right hand?" The monk thought, "Oh, what do I do now?" Then he thought, "Wait, I just took the Bodhisattva Vow. What an opportunity!" So he took a sword in his left hand and cut off his right hand. Very politely, he picked it up with his left hand and offered it to the Brahmin who became furious. He said, "I will not accept your generosity. To offer me something with your left hand is so disrespectful!" Then he left. So here was this monk standing at the crossroads, holding his severed right hand in his left hand, and the person for whom he had severed his hand was unwilling to accept it. Imagine that. That's why we call people who take this vow "Bodhisattvas."

THE BODHISATTVA VOW CEREMONY

Once you have taken this vow, you are a Bodhisattva. You have become sons and daughters of the Buddha's mind. Generally speaking, it is said that the Buddha had three types of children. There was Rahula, his physical son, the son of his body; the Shravakas who are the children of his speech; and the Bodhisattvas who are his dearest and closest children. For that reason, because you have become a child of the Buddha, the ceremony concludes with rejoicing in what you have done.

The ceremony consists of three parts: the preliminaries, the main body, and the conclusion. The preliminaries consist of reciting the *Seven Branch Supplication*. The reason for this is that it is essential to gather the accumulations of merit and wisdom in order to receive the vow. This is done symbolically at the time of the ceremony by the recitation of the *Seven Branch Supplication*. The main ceremony consists of repeating the words of the vows of Aspiration and Implementation Bodhicitta after the preceptor. The conclusion is the rejoicing liturgy and so forth.

The Seven Branch Supplication

We will begin by chanting the lineage supplication slowly and melodically in Tibetan. Then we will recite the *Seven Branch Supplication* in English as it will be easier for you to understand the meaning. We are taking the Vow in the Lineage of the Profound View which comes from Arya Manjushri to Nagarjuna, and so forth.

The preparation, or preliminaries

of this particular ceremony, is the accumulation of a vast amount of merit. In order to do this, we will recite the *Seven Branch Supplication* drawn from an aspiration called the *Aspiration to the Conduct of Excellence* which is found in the Green Tara text.

While reciting this supplication, please visualize all of the images you are chanting. Imagine countless forms of yourself making prostrations to countless Buddhas again and again. Further, imagine that all of the offering substances described are being emanated continuously. Think that you are admitting to and confessing all of your various unwholesome actions and that you are revealing your obscurations. Rejoice in the merit of ordinary beings and of the Shravakas, Pratyekabuddhas, Bodhisattvas and Buddhas. Exhort all of the teachers in the ten directions throughout the universe to teach, to turn the wheel of dharma. Request them all to remain for the benefit of beings and not to pass into nirvana. Dedicate this entire accumulation of merit to all sentient beings while doing these visualizations again and again, throughout the recitation. In this case, most of the offerings will be made through visualizations as described in the text.

In order to support our visualization, we've added a little bit to the offerings on the shrine. It is the intention of the text that one should offer one's favorite possession, that to which one is most attached, when requesting the Bodhisattva Vow. This is done in order to declare oneself a server of all sentient beings. One is giving up what one most enjoys, or that to which one is most attached, for the benefit of all beings.

With body, speech and mind, I pay homage to all those lions of humanity, as many as there are, without exception, who arise in the worlds of the ten directions and the three times. Through the power of this aspiration to excellent conduct, may I see in my mind all the Victors and bow to them with as many bodies as there are particles in all realms. On each particle, I imagine as many Buddhas as there are particles, surrounded by Bodhisattvas. In that way, I imagine the dharmadhatu totally filled with Victors. With all the sounds of inexhaustible oceans of song, I fully express the qualities of all the Victors. I praise all Sugatas.

I offer those Victors sacred flowers, holy garlands, cymbals, ointments, the best of parasols, the finest of lamps and sacred incense. I offer those Victors sacred fabrics, the finest of scents, heaps of medicinal powders equal in size to Mount Meru, and particularly excellent realms. I also imagine presenting to those Victors whatever offerings are unexcelled and vast. Through the power of faith in excellent conduct, I pay homage and present offerings to all Victors.

I confess individually all harmful actions I have done with body, speech and mind under the power of attachment, aversion, and bewilderment.

*I rejoice in all the merit of all
the Victors of the ten
directions, of the Bodhisattvas
and Pratyekabuddhas, of
those training and beyond
training, and of all beings.*

*I exhort all the lamps of
the ten directions who
have attained passionless
Buddhahood through the
stages of awakening, all
those protectors, to turn the
unsurpassable wheel of the
dharma.*

*With palms fully joined, I
request those wishing to
demonstrate passing into
nirvana to abide for as many
kalpas as there are particles
in all realms, for the benefit
and happiness of all beings.*

*I dedicate all virtue, however
slight, I have accumulated*

through homage, offering, confession, rejoicing, exhortation, and requesting, to awakening.

The Bodhisattva Vow

For the actual vow, one should visualize in the sky in front all the Buddhas and Bodhisattvas. This means that one thinks that all the Buddhas and Bodhisattvas are actually present and witnessing your taking of the Bodhisattva Vow. Try especially to generate a sense of the presence of Buddha Shakyamuni in the middle of the sky in front of you. He is surrounded by many Buddhas and Bodhisattvas, particularly the eight foremost heart sons such as Manjushri, Chenrezig, and so forth, as well as all of the lamas in the Kagyu lineage. In the presence of these, repeat the words of the vow after the preceptor.

The first half of the Bodhisattva Vow is actually the Mahayana Refuge. One says, "Until the very essence of awakening, I go for refuge to the Buddhas, the Dharma, and also the Sangha." The second half of the vow is the generation of the Bodhicitta of Aspiration and Implementation. The liturgy for this says, "In exactly the same way as the Buddhas of the past have generated Bodhicitta, which is the intention to attain supreme awakening, so do I, today, generate that same intention. And just as all the Buddhas of the past have trained in the path of awakening, which is the Six Paramitas, so do I, from today onward, begin to train in this path."

So now please repeat the vow after me. As you recite it in Tibetan, you can read the English transliteration and follow the meaning:

བྱང་ཆུབ་སྙིང་པོར་མཆིས་ཀྱི་བར།།

Jang Ch'up Nying Por Ch'i Kyi Bar

Until reaching the essence of
enlightenment,

སངས་རྒྱས་རྣམས་ལ་སྐྱབས་སུ་མཆི།།

Sang Gye Nam La Kyap Su Ch'i

I go for refuge to the Buddhas.

ཆོས་དང་བྱང་ཆུབ་སེམས་དཔའ་ཡི།།

Ch'ö Dang Jang Ch'up Sem Pa Yi

Also to the dharma and the assembly
of Bodhisattvas,

ཚོགས་ལའང་དེ་བཞིན་སྐྱབས་སུ་མཆི།།

Ts'ok Laang De Zhin Kyap Su Ch'i

I go for Refuge.

ཇི་ལྟར་སྔོན་གྱི་བདེ་གཤེགས་ཀྱིས།།

Ji Tar Ngön Gyi De Shek Kyi

Just as the former Sugatas

བྱང་ཆུབ་ཐུགས་ནི་བསྐྱེད་པ་དང་།།

Jang Ch'up T'uk Ni Kye Pa Dang

Generated the mind of enlightenment and

བྱང་ཆུབ་སེམས་དཔའི་བསླབ་པ་ལ།།

Jang Ch'up Sem Pai Lap Pa La

Dwelled in the trainings of a Bodhisattva

དེ་དག་རིམ་བཞིན་གནས་པ་ལྟར།།

De Dak Rim Zhin Ne Pa Tar

In accordance with the stages,

དེ་བཞིན་འགྲོ་ལ་ཕན་དོན་དུ།།

De Zhin Dro La P'en Dön Du

Similarly, in order to help sentient beings

བྱང་ཆུབ་སེམས་ནི་བསྐྱེད་བགྱི་ཞིང་།།

Jang Ch'up Sem Ni Kye Gyi Zhing

I will generate the mind of enlightenment and

དེ་བཞིན་དུ་ནི་བསླབ་པ་ལ་ལ་འང་། །

De Zhin Du Ni Lap Pa Laang

Train also in the trainings

རིམ་པ་བཞིན་དུ་བསླབ་པར་བགྱི། །

Rim Pa Zhin Du Lap Par Gyi

In accordance with the stages.

The actual generating of Bodhicitta and receiving of the Vow is now completed. Please rest evenly in the Bodhicitta you have generated.

Conclusion

The concluding part of the ceremony begins with your rejoicing in what you have done. The meaning of what is repeated here is the recognition that now, having taken the Bodhisattva Vow, your birth as a human being is meaningful. It is a recognition of the excellence of how you are leading your life and rejoicing in that.

Think that by taking this Bodhisattva Vow, "Today I have become a child of the Buddha. I have become a Bodhisattva and I will remain such from today onward. I will practice and conduct myself in a manner which is concordant with what I have become; in a manner that is concordant with the family I have entered." One rejoices in one's own taking of the vow. This is traditionally done in the same way, by repetition. So, please repeat the following words of rejoicing:

Today my life is fruitful. I have obtained a precious human existence and am born into the family of the Buddha; now I am a child of the Buddha.

From now on, I will only do activities appropriate to the lineage, so that no stain will come to this pure, faultless, noble family.

Today, in the presence of all the refuge, I invite all beings to enjoy happiness until they have reached Buddhahood. May the gods, demi-gods, and all other beings rejoice!

Bodhicitta is precious. Those who have not given birth to it, may they give birth. Those who have given birth, may their Bodhicitta not diminish, but increase further and further.

May they not be separated from Bodhicitta but be fully committed to Bodhisattva actions. May they be accepted by the Buddhas.

May they abandon all negative actions.

May all the good wishes of Bodhisattvas for the benefit of sentient beings be accomplished. May the intentions of such protectors bring happiness and prosperity to all beings.

May all sentient beings be happy. May the lower realms be emptied forever. May the earnest aspirations of Bodhisattvas of all stages be accomplished.

May all sentient beings have happiness and the cause of happiness.
May they be free from both suffering and the cause of suffering.

May they never be separated from the highest bliss, which is without suffering. May they come to rest in the great impartiality, which is free of attachment and aversion to those near and far.

What you've just said is that you have invited all beings, such as gods, humans, demons and others, to rely upon you. You have said, "From this moment onward, I take full responsibility for your welfare. Relax. Enjoy my service. Give me your orders, and I'll try to fill them."

RESTORING BODHICITTA

There are two primary means of repairing Bodhicitta when you slip. These ways of admitting the slip and restoring Bodhicitta have been taught in the sutras. One way is to recite the names of thirty-five particular Buddhas; and then admit the slip. There is actually something very specific that you recite which is not very long. It is part of a sutra called the *Sutra of Three Aggregates*. It is readily available in the West. Most people simply call it the *Thirty-five Buddhas* but its actual name is the *Sutra of Three Aggregates*. That's one method. If you recite this every day, then it will restore the Bodhicitta from any slips that occur.

The second method for restoration is meditation on selflessness. It is said that meditation on selflessness, on emptiness, is the most profound and effective way of restoring Bodhicitta that has been impaired. In order to do that, there is the custom of reciting the *Heart Sutra* on a daily basis. Daily recitation of the *Heart Sutra*, which is a framework for the recollection of emptiness, is an effective method of restoring impaired Bodhicitta. It is recommended that you recite either the *Sutra of Three Aggregates* or the *Heart Sutra* on a daily basis. However, the most important thing is that you actually try to practice the Six Perfections.

DEDICATION OF MERIT

*By whatever boundless merit
  we have attained
Through hearing this precious,
  genuine dharma of the
  supreme yana,
May all beings become a
  stainless vessel
Of the precious, genuine
  dharma of the supreme yana.*

This was written by Asanga.

*By this virtue, may all beings
Perfect the accumulations of
  merit and wisdom
And achieve the two genuine
  kayas
Arising from merit and wisdom.*

This was written by Nagarjuna.

That's it. Welcome to the world
of Bodhisattvas. Welcome to the
world of Warriors.

BIOGRAPHICAL INFORMATION

Dzogchen Ponlop Rinpoche

Dzogchen Ponlop Rinpoche, acknowledged as one of the foremost scholars and educators of his generation in the Nyingma and Kagyu schools of Tibetan Buddhism, was born at Rumtek Monastery (Dharma Chakra Center) in Sikkim, India in 1965, where he was recognized by His Holiness the 16th Gyalwang Karmapa and enthroned in 1968.

Rinpoche received Buddhist refuge and bodhisattva vows from His Holiness Karmapa at an early age. He received the complete teachings and empowerments of the Kagyu and Nyingma traditions from His Holiness Karmapa, His Holiness Dilgo Khyentsé, Rinpoche, Khenpo Tsultrim Gyamtso Rinpoche and others. In May, 1990, Rinpoche graduated from the Karma Shri Nalanda Institute for

Higher Buddhist Studies as an Acharya, or Master of Buddhist Philosophy. He also studied comparative religions at Columbia University in New York City.

Rinpoche is fluent in the English language and is an accomplished calligrapher, visual artist and poet. Known for his sharp intellect, humor, and the lucidity of his teaching, Rinpoche uses his deep understanding of both Eastern and Western cultures to teach throughout the world.

Nitartha *international*

In 1994, to assist in the integration of computer technology with traditional Tibetan scholarship, Rinpoche founded Nitartha *international*, a non-profit education corporation based in New York City. Nitartha uses computer technologies to support Tibetan studies and education, and preserves the ancient literature of Tibet in computerized formats.

In addition to his work in traditional Tibetan educational institutions, Rinpoche works actively to develop and adapt traditional Tibetan education curriculums for Western audiences. In 1995 he helped establish Nitartha Institute in North America, which provides a focused Tibetan studies program for Westerners.

Nalandabodhi

In 1997, Rinpoche founded Nalandabodhi, an association of Buddhist meditation and study centers to preserve the genuine lineage of the Nyingma and Kagyu Schools of Tibetan Buddhism. The spiritual head of Nalandabodhi is Rinpoche's main teacher, Khenpo Tsultrim Gyamtso Rinpoche.

In 1998, at the request of His Holiness, the Seventeenth Gyalwa Karmapa, Rinpoche became director of the Kamalashila Institute, the primary Kagyu educational and practice center in Germany. Rinpoche is also a regular visiting professor at Naropa University in Boulder, Colorado.

Additional information on the
activities of
Dzogchen Ponlop Rinpoche
can be found at
www.nalandabodhi.org
and
www.nitartha.org.

In Canada, please contact:
Nalandabodhi Foundation
Post Office Box 2355
Vancouver, British Columbia
Canada V6B 3W5

In the United States, please contact:
Nalandabodhi
5501 Seventeenth Avenue N.E.
Seattle, Washington 98105

Nitartha *international*
1914 Bigelow Avenue North, Suite 5
Seattle, WA 98109

BOOKS FROM
SIDDHI PUBLICATIONS

Entering the Path
The Refuge Vow
Dzogchen Ponlop, Rinpoche

Turning Towards Liberation
Dzogchen Ponlop, Rinpoche

The Essence of Benefit and Joy:
A Method for the Saving of Lives
Jamgon Kongtrul Lodro Thaye